EAU CLAIRE DISTRICT LIBRARY
6528 East Main Street
P.O. Box 328
EAU CLAIRE, MI 49111

J
921
N

W9-AYO-149

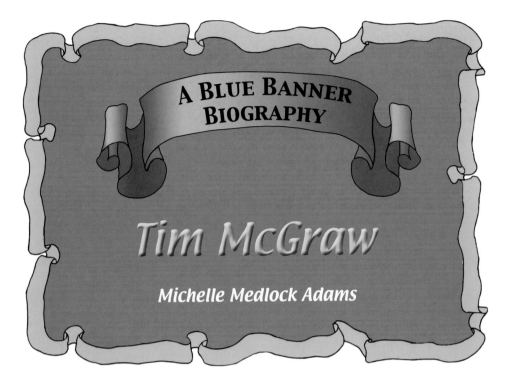

A BLUE BANNER BIOGRAPHY

Tim McGraw

Michelle Medlock Adams

PUBLISHERS

P.O. Box 196
Hockessin, Delaware 19707
Visit us on the web: www.mitchelllane.com
Comments? email us: mitchelllane@mitchelllane.com

EAU CLAIRE DISTRICT LIBRARY

T 138636

Mitchell Lane PUBLISHERS

Copyright © 2007 by Mitchell Lane Publishers. All rights reserved. No part of this book may be reproduced without written permission from the publisher. Printed and bound in the United States of America.

Printing	2	3	4	5	6	7	8	9

Blue Banner Biographies

Alan Jackson	Alicia Keys	Allen Iverson
Ashanti	Ashlee Simpson	Ashton Kutcher
Avril Lavigne	Beyoncé	Bow Wow
Britney Spears	Christina Aguilera	Christopher Paul Curtis
Clay Aiken	Condoleezza Rice	Daniel Radcliffe
Derek Jeter	Eminem	Eve
50-Cent	Gwen Stefani	Ice Cube
Jamie Foxx	Ja Rule	Jay-Z
Jennifer Lopez	J. K. Rowling	Jodie Foster
Justin Berfield	Kate Hudson	Kelly Clarkson
Kenny Chesney	Lance Armstrong	Lindsay Lohan
Mariah Carey	Mario	Mary-Kate and Ashley Olsen
Melissa Gilbert	Michael Jackson	Miguel Tejada
Missy Elliott	Nelly	Orlando Bloom
Paris Hilton	P. Diddy	Peyton Manning
Queen Latifah	Rita Williams-Garcia	Ritchie Valens
Ron Howard	Rudy Giuliani	Sally Field
Selena	Shirley Temple	**Tim McGraw**
Usher		

Library of Congress Cataloging-in-Publication Data
Adams, Michelle Medlock.
    Tim McGraw / by Michelle Medlock Adams.
        p. cm. — (Blue banner biographies)
    Includes bibliographical references (p.), discography, and index.
    ISBN 1-58415-501-9 (library bound : alk. paper)
    1. McGraw, Tim—Juvenile literature. 2. Country musicians—United States—Biography—Juvenile literature. I. Title. II. Blue banner biography.
ML3930.M38A65 2006
782.421642092 — dc22   2005036694

ISBN-10: 1-58415-501-9   ISBN-13: 978-1-58415-501-0

ABOUT THE AUTHOR: Award-winning journalist **Michelle Medlock Adams** has published more than 3,000 articles in newspapers and magazines around the country, such as *Writer's Digest*, *Today's Christian Woman*, *Brio*, and *American Cheerleader Magazine*. She has also authored 26 books, including her award-winning picture book, *Conversations on the Ark*. For Mitchell Lane Publishers, she has written *Jamie Lynn Spears*, *Brandi Chastain*, and *Kenny Chesney*. She and her husband, Jeff, and their two daughters, Abby and Allyson, make their home in Texas with their three miniature dachshunds.

PHOTO CREDITS: Cover—Peter Kramer/Getty Images; p. 4—Ron Wolfson/WireImage; p. 6—Chuck Burton/AP Photo; p. 8—Ed Rode/WireImage; p. 12—Jim Smeal/WireImage; p. 16—Dan Currier/AP Photo/The News-Star; pp. 18, 21—Thomas S. England/Time Life Pictures/Getty Images; p. 23—Steve Granitz/WireImage; p. 26—William E. Amatucci Jr./WireImage.

PUBLISHER'S NOTE: The following story has been thoroughly researched, and to the best of our knowledge represents a true story. While every possible effort has been made to ensure accuracy, the publisher will not assume liability for damages caused by inaccuracies in the data, and makes no warranty on the accuracy of the information contained herein. This story has not been authorized or endorsed by Tim McGraw.

CONTENTS

Country music star Tim McGraw performs at the Academy of Country Music Awards Show in 2005, during which he won Single and Song of the Year for "Live Like You Were Dying."

The Star Who Shines
Inside and Out

When Hurricane Katrina tore through the Southern part of the United States, destroying everything in its path, in August 2005, the nation watched in horror and heartbreak — especially those who called the South home.

Born in Delhi, Louisiana, country superstar Tim McGraw took Hurricane Katrina's rampage very personally. Immediately, he wanted to help those who had lost their homes, their businesses, and their family members.

"I am heartbroken by the devastation caused by Hurricane Katrina in my home state," McGraw declared in a press release issued August 31, 2005. "Like so many Americans I am watching the news reports with great sadness. But it's at times like these that each of us must work together to provide lifesaving aid to those in terrible need. I sincerely encourage everyone to support the American Red Cross, government efforts and others in the non-profit community with this historically unprecedented undertaking."

Big-hearted Tim McGraw (center) gets an up-close look at a Louisiana trailer park devastated by Hurricane Katrina with Lt. Gov. Mitch Landrieu (right).

McGraw, along with a host of Hollywood and music celebrities, joined efforts with the American Red Cross and NBC to put on a concert in support of Hurricane Katrina victims that aired on Friday, September 2. It was broadcast in more than 95 countries, raising much-needed money. The telethon featured McGraw, Harry Connick Jr., Wynton Marsalis, and Leonardo DiCaprio, to name a few. After the concert, McGraw and several other celebrities signed a Gibson guitar to be auctioned off on eBay to further benefit the victims of Hurricane Katrina.

Tim McGraw fans weren't surprised that their favorite country music star jumped in to help the hurricane victims. After all, he's always had a big heart—a star who shines inside and out.

In fact, he served four years on the American Red Cross celebrity cabinet. And he served as the National Spokesperson for State Farm's Neighbors Give Life national blood drive campaign.

Tim McGraw is no stranger to tough times. He didn't have a storybook childhood. He didn't grow up in a big house with rich parents. In fact, he had to grow up fast when he learned some life-changing news at age eleven.

Tim found out that his dad was the famous baseball pitcher Frank Edwin "Tug" McGraw. Tim couldn't believe it.

That's when he learned that Horace Smith, the man he had called dad since before he could talk, wasn't really his father. Instead, Tim found out that his dad was the famous baseball pitcher Frank Edwin "Tug" McGraw. Tim couldn't believe it. He had a baseball card with Tug's picture on it hanging in his room, but he never knew that Tug was his father until that day in 1978.

According to Tim's mother, Betty Trimble, in her book *A Mother's Story* (published in 1996), she had hoped she wouldn't have to tell Tim the truth about his father until he was at least sixteen. But when Tim was in elementary school, he found his birth certificate while searching for a photo for a school project.

She remembers that day well.

Tim called his mom at work and begged her to come home right away. Sensing the sadness in Tim's voice, Betty left work early and hurried home. She found her two

Country music superstar Tim McGraw and his mother, Betty Trimble, take in Friday Night Lights *at the Tennessee movie premiere. McGraw has an acting role in this 2004 football movie.*

daughters outside, playing ball with the babysitter, but Tim was nowhere to be found.

Then she found him. He was lying facedown on his bed. "What's wrong?" Betty asked.

He sat up and handed her a sheet of paper. It was his birth certificate, which she had kept hidden in a metal box in her closet.

"I had to have an old picture for school," Tim explained. "We're writing about things we liked to do when we were little and I was going to write about riding horses with Dad and needed a picture. But he ain't my dad, is he?"

Betty and Tim both cried as she told him how sorry she was that he had found out about his father in that way. She said, "I was planning on telling you when you were older. Horace is not your dad. Tug McGraw is your father."

Tim kept asking, "Are you sure, Mom? The famous baseball player? The guy on my wall is my dad?"

She told Tim how she had met his father and how Tug had chosen a career in baseball over a family.

"Does he know where I am and have I ever seen him?" Tim asked his mom.

"No, you haven't ever seen him; nor has he ever seen you," she explained. "He knows about you. . . . I love you, Tim! I chose you. Do you hate me for not telling you?"

Mother and son shared a sad afternoon together. They went for a drive and discussed the situation for hours.

"Mom, will I ever get to meet my real dad?"

> *Deep down, Tim knew he'd one day meet his real father. . . . But he had no idea that he would become even more famous than his sports celebrity father.*

Betty wasn't sure how to answer that question.

"I don't know, sweetie. I just don't know," she said.

Deep down, Tim knew he'd one day meet his real father, and he was right. But he had no idea that he would become even more famous than his sports celebrity father. Tim would one day become a country music superstar.

The Early Years

*E*lizabeth Ann "Betty" Dagostino, a good Catholic Italian girl, and Tug McGraw, a professional baseball player, had a brief love affair in the late 1960s. Even though their love didn't last, their union produced a child. Samuel Timothy McGraw came into this world on May 1, 1967. He was born in Delhi, Louisiana.

Betty was still in high school when she became pregnant with Tim, and Tug was playing baseball around the country. He made it clear he wanted no part in raising a family, so Betty was left to raise Tim on her own. One cousin tried to tell her it would be better for her to give her child up for adoption, but Betty just couldn't. In *A Mother's Story*, she wrote:

> "I couldn't even think about giving my baby up. Maybe it would be right for someone else, but not me. This was my child no matter what the circumstances. I loved this baby already. I wanted to see it grow up and I wanted to be there for this child. . . . I wanted a

boy and wanted him to look just like Tug McGraw. . . .
I wanted my son to be strong, handsome, and
intelligent. I wanted him to grow up to be 'somebody'
just to show Tug McGraw. I would pray for God to
make him special. . . ."

Betty's prayers would eventually
be answered. Tim would become
somebody—somebody very special.

Betty worked part-time at a
garment factory, and her mother
(Tim's grandmother) watched baby
Tim while Betty worked. Then Tim's
grandparents divorced, so Betty had
to get another part-time job as a
waitress to help with the mounting
bills. Finally she was able to get a full-
time job at the bus station café in
Rayville, Louisiana. That job paid
more than her other two jobs together,
but money was still very tight. After
paying all the weekly expenses, Betty
would have only five dollars left over.

Betty made most of her own
clothes and bought most of Tim's
outfits at the dollar store. They didn't
have many possessions, but they had

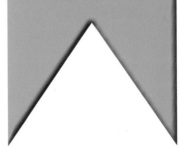

Betty's prayers would eventually be answered. Tim would become somebody—somebody very special.

a lot of love in that little apartment. Every night, she rocked
Tim to sleep, singing songs from the sound track for *My Fair
Lady*. She knew every word to every song, and he liked them
all. Tim especially liked to hear Elvis Presley sing. Whenever
Elvis came on the radio, he would get very excited and bounce
around in his seat.

When Tim was less than a year old, Betty began dating
Horace. He was a nice thirty-year-old man who wanted to

Tim McGraw poses with three very important ladies in his life – his mother and sisters, Tracey and Sandy – at the 1995 Academy of Country Music Awards.

take care of Betty and Tim, and they certainly needed someone to help. Horace asked Betty to marry him and even offered to adopt Tim, but Betty wasn't sure she should say yes. It was so soon. She barely knew him, yet he seemed kind. She liked him, but she wasn't sure she loved him. After several months, he finally convinced her to marry him, but she didn't agree to Tim's adoption. She wanted Tim to keep Tug's last name. She said that one day she would tell Tim about his real father.

Soon after Betty and Horace got married, Betty discovered that Horace had a very bad temper. He would get angry and hit her. He gave her a black eye one night, and he spanked Tim too often. Still, Betty was determined to make the marriage work. She cooked dinner and had it ready when he came home from work—exactly at 5:15 P.M. Horace had good and bad days, but the bad days were really bad.

Not too long after they were married, Betty found out she was going to have another baby. She was worried that Horace would be angry if she told him, but he wasn't. He was actually happy about the pregnancy. He wanted to have a boy of his own. Secretly, Betty wished for a baby sister for Tim.

It seemed that everything was going okay—until Horace began drinking too much. He hit Betty again, knocking her to the floor. She was worried that her fall would hurt her unborn baby, but the doctor said that she and the baby were fine. On September 9, 1968, Tracey Catherine Smith was born, and Tim had a baby sister after all. Tim liked being a big brother. He helped rock his new sister. He sang "Rock-a-bye Baby" and his favorite Elvis song, "Teddy Bear."[2]

> *Tim liked being a big brother. He helped rock his new sister. He sang "Rock-a-bye Baby" and his favorite Elvis song, "Teddy Bear."*

Even as a toddler, Tim showed promise as a singer. He was destined to be a superstar.

EAU CLAIRE DISTRICT LIBRARY

The Singing Cowboy

When Tim was three and Tracey was two, the family moved out to the country. If Horace would take care of the landlord's horses, they'd only have to pay half the normal rent. They agreed to the arrangement and moved. Betty didn't like being so far from town, but Tim loved it. That year, he became a real cowboy. His aunt let him ride their Shetland pony. It was just the right size for Tim.

"He would ride him in the yard all day playing cowboys," Betty wrote in her book. "Timmy was getting good at riding. Horace kept saying he was going to put him on a big horse soon; that scared me to death."

That July, Betty became pregnant again. She was twenty-two years old when she had her third child. On April 7, 1971, Sandra Estelle Smith was born, and Tim had another little sister to play with.

Horace still got angry sometimes and hit Betty. Still, she tried to make the marriage work, since she now had three little children to take care of.

Not long after Sandra was born, the family moved again—to a town named Jigger. This time, they moved to a house that had actually been used as a barn. In fact, it still had hay in it when they moved in. Betty worked hard to make it a nice home for her family. They adjusted to their new surroundings, and they started going to church.

"The kids liked the Pentecostal church. Kids didn't have to sit still there, and they loved the singing. Timmy, Tracey, and Joey, a neighbor's son, would sing trios occasionally in church. Timmy loved it," Betty wrote in her book.

Eventually the family moved again—to another town in Louisiana. Because of Horace's frequent job changes, they moved seven times during Tim's early years. At this home in the country, Horace started teaching Tim to ride big horses, and Tim was a natural. He was on his way to becoming a real cowboy.

Horace, Betty, and the kids moved yet again, and Tim and Tracey started school. Soon Tim's musical talents were recognized. In second grade, he was chosen to be the announcer for a recital. He sang "The Battle Hymn of the Republic."

"Timmy was very shy until he got on stage, but once there, he would loosen up," Betty wrote. "Afterward, he was embarrassed at everyone fussing over him."

Not only was Tim gifted at music, but he also discovered he could play baseball—just like his real dad. When he was

Eventually the family moved again—to another town in Louisiana. They moved seven times during Tim's early years.

Like father, like son—Tim McGraw has always loved baseball like his late dad, professional baseball player Tug McGraw. In fact, Tim went to college on a baseball scholarship. Now he plays for fun. Here, Tim plays shortstop while his wife, Faith Hill, stands on second base.

old enough to play Little League, Betty saved up her money to buy him a glove and a ball. His cleats were hand-me-downs, but Tim didn't care. He found out he was good, really good.

From that time on, music and sports competed for his attention. They were a great escape for Tim—an escape from the stress of his home life. Horace was still hitting Betty occasionally, and that was hard on the whole family. Then the unthinkable happened.

Betty found out she had cancer. She was only twenty-seven, and Tim was still in grade school. He needed his mom.

They were buddies. She didn't tell Tim she had cancer right away. She didn't want him to worry. She just told the kids that she was sick and had to go to the hospital for a while. Betty had surgery and radiation, and the doctors were able to get rid of all the cancer. The family was very happy with the good news, but Betty was still worried. She began thinking, "What if I had died? I wouldn't want Horace to raise the children. They needed me."

Several months after Betty's surgery, Tim's music teacher stopped by their home and told them the little theater in town was putting on *The Music Man*. She wanted Tim to try out for the lead part in that musical. She was sure he would get it! Tim was one of six boys who tried out for the part. He sang "The Battle Hymn of the Republic," and by the time he got to the second line, the director had made his decision. Tim was in! When Tim finished his song, everyone stood and applauded. At nine years old, he was a star. He had experienced a breakthrough.

Betty had her own breakthrough that same year. Horace got mad one night and started to hit her with a chair. For the first time, she fought back. She hit Horace over and over again until he begged her to stop. She was no longer afraid of him. She put Tim and his sisters in the car and left Horace for good. Betty divorced Horace when Tim was nine, Tracey was eight, and Sandy was six. They had broken free. They were ready for a new beginning.

When Tim finished his song, everyone stood and applauded. At nine years old, he was a star. He had experienced a breakthrough.

Finding His Way

Money was scarcer than ever once the divorce was final. Betty, Tim, and his little sisters lived on a tight family budget, but they still had fun. They did crafts, made music, and laughed a lot. But once Tim found out that Tug McGraw was his real father, he was very upset. He wanted to meet his real dad. He wanted to know if Tug would like him, maybe even love him. Betty contacted Tug and told him how Tim had found his birth certificate. The truth was out. They made arrangements for a meeting when Tug's team played in Houston two weeks later.

Tim was very excited about meeting his father.

When they arrived in Houston, Betty called Tug. An hour later, they met in the hotel lobby. Tim and Tug shook hands and sat down to talk. Tug was nice to Tim, but he told him not to refer to him as his father. "Just say we're friends," Tug coached Tim.

Tug took Tim to batting practice and had the entire team sign a baseball for him. Tim even got the chance to play catch with is favorite Philly player—Greg Luzinski. Tug also gave

Tim and Tug McGraw share a fun moment together in 1994, exchanging their favorite hats during a photo opportunity.

Tim a Phillies hat. They had a nice visit, but that was it. When Tim tried to contact his father by writing letters to the Phillies' office, those letters were ignored. Tim tried to call his dad a couple of times, too, but those calls weren't returned. Tim saw his father only on TV or in the sports pages. That would have to be enough. He went back and forth, calling himself Timmy Smith and then Tim McGraw. He wasn't sure he should use the last name of a man who wouldn't be his father.

> *Tim was a good student, too. He made straight A's. He had been offered several college scholarships, and he had accepted one for baseball.*

Life went on, and Tim got interested in basketball, 4-H, and girls. At age fifteen, Tim began riding in rodeos. He was a great rider. Of course, he had always been athletic. At age seventeen, Tim was already six feet tall.

Tim was a good student, too. He made straight A's. He had been offered several college scholarships, and he had accepted one for baseball. He planned to attend the University of Louisiana at Monroe, also called Northeast Louisiana University, and study sports medicine. Tim graduated from his high school as salutatorian, meaning he had the second highest grade-point average in his high school class.

Right before he went to college, Tim and Tug got together once again. Tug agreed to pay for college. He even called from time to time, and he arranged for Tim to meet his stepmother and step siblings—a stepsister named Carrie and a stepbrother named Mark. Tim and Tug had begun a relationship, but it was slow going.

Tim basically taught himself how to play guitar when he was eighteen. His musical ability was a gift. He played solo in regional nightspots while attending the university, but he wanted to pursue music full-time. Sure, he was having fun at college as a member of the Pi Kappa Alpha fraternity, but his heart was elsewhere. Tim dropped out of college in 1989 and

Tim McGraw found out he was better at more than just sports. He was also good at playing music.

headed to Nashville on the same day his country music hero Keith Whitley passed away. Tim sang in Nashville clubs for a few years before landing a recording deal in 1992 with Curb Records. His first single, "Welcome to the Club" did okay. It was a minor hit. His first album, *Tim McGraw*, saw some success in 1993. Tim had two hits, "Memory Lane" and "Two Steppin' Mind."

> *Tim met a woman who would change his life forever—Faith Hill. He toured with Faith in 1996. . . . They fell in love that year, and got married . . .*

He was doing what he loved, and eventually, he knew, he would make it. His mother had always believed in him, and Tim believed in himself. His big break came in 1994 with the release of "Indian Outlaw." It was a popular song with the fans, but it was quite controversial because of its subject matter. Some Native American groups were angry over the lyrics. Some radio stations even banned the song. But even bad publicity can be good for a celebrity. It certainly got Tim's name out there, and his popularity grew. In 1995, his album *All I Want* became a hit, and his fans grew in number. Then Tim met a woman who would change his life forever — Faith Hill. He toured with Faith in 1996. Almost immediately, Tim and Faith became a couple. They fell in love that year, and got married on October 6, 1996. Tim had always been close with the women in his life — his mom and his sisters. Now, he had another woman to love. It was the beginning of a beautiful life of love, laughter, and lyrical magic.

Country superstar couple Faith Hill and Tim McGraw sport their matching Best Country Collaboration With Vocals awards at the Grammy Awards in 2006. They won for their song "Like We Never Loved At All."

A Lot to Live For

*T*he year 1996 proved to be a very good one for Tim McGraw. He not only married the love of his life, but he also watched his song "She Never Lets It Go To Her Heart" climb to number one on the country music charts. He was now a hit-making machine, a superstar, and a mainstream celebrity with a huge fan following. All of his mama's prayers had been answered in a big way. Tim McGraw truly was somebody very special.

Tim has had dozens of hits, and he has certainly made great music with his band, the Dancehall Doctors. He has also made great music with his wife, Faith Hill. They made something else, too—a daughter. Faith and Tim welcomed Gracie Katherine into the world on May 5, 1997. Then, on August 12, 1998, Faith gave birth to Maggie Elizabeth. And, on December 6, 2001, Audrey Caroline joined her two big sisters as the third child in their happy family.

Tim and Faith continue selling out arenas for concerts and making music that wins awards and the respect of their peers. Their songs have topped music charts and touched many hearts. Tim has consistently sold millions of copies of his albums.

"There's not really a recipe to selling albums," Tim said in an interview with Yahoo Music. "But nobody's going to buy a record if they don't believe that you believe what you're singing. People believe me; that's what I think I bring to my music. I sing songs that say what I would say if I was in that position."

That was certainly the case for Tim's hit single "Live Like You Were Dying."

"We were rehearsing when Tug was sick," Tim shared on his web site, www.timmcgraw.com. "And Tug died at the beginning of January [2004]. We were in the studio at the end of January, and we recorded this around 11 or 12 at night and everybody just poured a lot of heart and soul into it. I think you can hear that on the record."

Tim said the song was very personal to him. After years of being apart, Tug and Tim had finally formed a father/son friendship, so when Tug died of cancer, it was heartbreaking for Tim. "Live Like You Were Dying" seemed fitting to record just weeks after his dad's passing.

"This song is personal to a lot of people . . . ," Tim said in an interview with Yahoo Music. "It's such a great song, and everybody can take what they want out of it. And I think that this song more than anything is an affirmation of life."

Tim continues to sell out arenas, make number one records, win numerous awards, make movies (he had parts in *Friday Night Lights*, *Black Cloud*, and *Flicka*), and experience a

> *After years of being apart, Tim and Tug had finally formed a father/son friendship, so when Tug died of cancer, it was heartbreaking for Tim.*

Tim McGraw celebrates the moment while performing at halftime of the Dallas Cowboys versus the Washington Redskins Monday Night Football game in September 2004. It was a dream come true for the sports-loving country music star.

level of success his mama had prayed he would. He's doing things he never even imagined. In fact, ABC's Monday Night Football announced in the fall of 2005 that Tim would do musical halftime presentations throughout the football season. This unique arrangement joins Tim's love for music and sports. He's living his dream. But Tim is keeping his feet firmly planted on the ground. He knows that the most important thing in life is family. He adores all of his girls.

"As fast as it's moving, we know we've got the good life," Tim says on his web site. "We're very blessed, just very fortunate to have the things we have."

Tim has discovered he has a lot to live for, and he's basking in it every minute of every day.

2001 "Angry All the Time"
      "Grown Men Don't Cry"'
      "The Cowboy in Me"
2000 "My Next Thirty Years"
1999 "Please Remember Me"
      "Something Like That"
1998 "Where the Green Grass Grows"
1997 "Everywhere"
      "It's Your Love"
1996 "She Never Lets It Go to Her Heart"
1995 "I Like It, I Love It"
1994 "Don't Take the Girl"
      "Not a Moment Too Soon"
      "Indian Outlaw"

2006 Grammy: Vocal Collaboration with Faith Hill for "Like We
      Never Loved At All"
2005 ACM* Award: Single and Song of the Year; Grammy: Best
      Male Country Vocal Performance; CMT* Award: Most
      Inspiring Video—all for "Live Like You Were Dying"
2004 CMA* Award: Single of the Year for "Live Like You Were
      Dying" (two awards—one as artist, one as producer)
2003 American Music Awards: Favorite Male Country Artist in
      January and November
2002 American Music Awards: Best Country Album for Set This
      Circus Down and Favorite Country Artist

*ACM = Academy of Country Music; CMT = Country Music Television; CMA = Country
Music Association

2001   American Music Award: Favorite Male Country Artist; Grammy: Vocal Collaboration with Faith Hill for "Let's Make Love"; CMA Award: Entertainer of the Year

2000   CMA Award: Male Vocalist; ACM Award: Male Vocalist

1999   ACM Awards: Male Vocalist and Vocal Collaboration with Faith Hill for "Just To Hear You Say That You Love Me"; CMA Awards: Male Vocalist and Album of the Year for A Place In The Sun

1998   CMA Award: Album of the Year for Everywhere; ACM Awards: Single of the Year, Song of the Year, Video of the Year and Top Vocal Event for "It's Your Love" with Faith Hill

1997   CMT Awards: Male Artist of the Year, Video of the Year for "It's Your Love"; CMA Award: Vocal Event for "It's Your Love"

1995   American Music Award: Favorite New Country Artist

1994   CMT Award: Male Video Artist of the Year; ACM Awards: Album of the Year for Not A Moment Too Soon and Top New Male Vocalist

FURTHER READING

Gray, Scott. *Perfect Harmony*. New York: Ballantine Books, 1999.

McGraw, Tim, with Martin Huxley. *This Is Ours: Tim McGraw and the Dancehall Doctors*. New York: Atria Books, 2002.

Trimble, Betty "McMom." *A Mother's Story*. Nashville, Tennessee: D'Agostino/Dahlhauser/Ditmore Publishing, 1996.

Askmen.com, Tim McGraw Biography
http://www.askmen.com/men/entertainment_60/75c_tim_mcgraw.html

CMT.com. Tim McGraw
http://www.cmt.com/artists/az/mcgraw_tim/bio.jtml
Curb.com. "Tim McGraw"
http://curb.com
DiMartino, Dave. "A Lot to Live For," Yahoo Music Interviews, March
    10, 2005
http://music.yahoo.com/read/interview/14129756
GACTV.com. "Tim McGraw: Live Like You Were Dying"
http://www.gactv.com/artists/tim.html
Tim McGraw Official Web Site
www.timmcgraw.com/
Vh1.com. "Tim McGraw"
http://www.vh1.com/artists/az/mcgraw_tim/artist.jhtml

Works Consulted
Trimble, Betty "McMom." *A Mother's Story*. Nashville, Tennessee:
    D'Agostino/Dahlhauser/Ditmore Publishing, 1996.
Tim McGraw Awards
www.timmcgraw.com/news/awards/php
Tim McGraw Discography
www.timmcgraw.com/discog/discog.php?view=all
The Tug McGraw Foundation
http://www.tugmcgraw.com/HomePage.html
CMT.com — Tim McGraw
http://www.cmt.com/artists/az/mcgraw_tim/bio.jtml
"The Everyman Is Everywhere"
http://www.music.yahoo.com/read/interview/1230599
Tim McGraw Biography
www.timmcgraw.com/news/bio.php
"A Lot to Live For"
http://music.yahoo.com/read/interview/14129756
"Tim McGraw Partners With ABC's NFL"
http://www.timmcgraw.com/news/news/php?uid=370
"Tim McGraw to Headline NBC Concert in Support of Hurricane
    Katrina Victims"
http://www.timmcgraw.com/news/news.php?uid=385

INDEX

EAU CLAIRE DISTRICT LIBRARY